Contents

Why Teach Handwriting?

Handwriting is still an important life skill. Writing by hand ties in closely with the skills of reading and comprehending. Handwriting personalizes communication with others in a way that technological devices cannot. Neat, legible writing is a skill that students can take pride in throughout their lives.

Teacher Tips

• Teach in small groups of Modelled Cursive Writing sessions.

• Show students some words in both printing and cursive writing. Ask them to describe the similarities and differences. For example, in cursive writing the letters of a word are joined together, whereas in printing the letters of a word are separated.

• Point out that, in cursive writing, there is usually a beginning "tail," and an ending "tail." These "tails" are what join the letters of a word together.

• Demonstrate for students how, during cursive writing, the pencil should not be lifted from the paper until the word has been completed. Only a few letters, such as capital "T," do not connect to the rest of a word when cursive writing.

- Teach letters with a similar formation in clusters. For example,

a c d g	*h k*	*e f l*	*i j t*
r s u w	*b o v*	*m n x*	*p q y z*

- On chart paper or whiteboard, demonstrate the formation of the cursive letter being taught in writing. Describe your movements out loud as you write. Focus on the proper alignment, shape, and slant of your writing.

- Invite students to "write" the letter in the air with big arm movements.

- Use the practise sheets found in this resource as immediate follow-up to each lesson. Have students circle their best letter on each line as a form of self-assessment. Encourage students to express why they chose their best letter.

- As students are practising their cursive writing skills, make sure to reinforce good posture habits. Slouching will create unnecessary strain on students' young spines.

- You may wish to play classical music to create an inspiring atmosphere as students practise their cursive writing skills.

Motivation

Consider these ideas to motivate students to practise their cursive writing skills, see progress, feel pride in accomplishment, and have a product to show for their hard work:

- Keep students' work organized in a portfolio, folder, or scrapbook, or bind practice pages into a book for each student.

- As students complete cursive writing lessons successfully, have them colour in their personal completion chart provided in this resource.

- For proficient cursive writers, provide short poems and nursery rhymes to copy. Encourage students to illustrate their pages and bind them together to make a book.

General Support

The classroom environment, and your attention to individual needs, can promote the development of good handwriting. Here are some tips and suggestions for helping students learn to write legibly:

• Display the cursive alphabet in the classroom where all students can see it. Consider attaching photocopies of the alphabet, with letter formation, to desks or tables for students who may need it.

• Model legible writing at every opportunity.

• Remind students to hold their writing tools properly.

• Ensure that pencils are sharpened before use.

• If you notice some students having difficulty with specific letters, call them together for small group or individual instruction or review.

Encouraging Fine Motor Control and Finger Muscle Strength

Provide activities that increase fine motor control and finger muscle strength, such as

• modelling clay to roll small balls, or create sculptures with details

• art projects that involve using crayons, finger paints, scissors, or tearing paper

• building blocks that snap together

• paper clips to string together

• puzzles

• lacing or stitching cards

• paper to cut, paste, and fold

Monitoring Progress

• Use the rubric in this book to assess students' learning. Encourage students to self-assess their cursive writing according to the rubric provided.

Cursive Alphabet—Lower-case Letters

Trace the lower-case letters.

Cursive Alphabet—Upper-case Letters

Trace the upper-case letters.

Trace and write. Circle your best 𝒶 or 𝑎 on each line.

𝒶 𝒶 𝒶 𝒶 𝒶 𝒶 𝒶

𝒶

𝒶

Allosaurus

𝑎 𝑎 𝑎 𝑎 𝑎 𝑎 𝑎

𝑎

𝑎

add

aa

Trace and write. Circle your best *B* or *b* on each line.

Trace and write. Circle your best $\mathcal{B}$ or b on each line.

$\mathcal{B}$ $\mathcal{B}$ $\mathcal{B}$ $\mathcal{B}$ $\mathcal{B}$ $\mathcal{B}$ $\mathcal{B}$

$\mathcal{B}$

$\mathcal{B}$

Brian

b b b b b b b b

b

b

bat

boy

$\mathcal{B}$ $\mathcal{B}$ $\mathcal{B}$ $\mathcal{B}$ $\mathcal{B}$ $\mathcal{B}$ $\mathcal{B}$

$\mathcal{B}$

$\mathcal{B}$

Barosaurus

b b b b b b b b

b

b

bus

bed

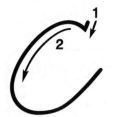

Trace and write. Circle your best C or c on each line.

Centrosaurus

cat

cup

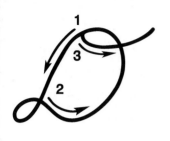 

Trace and write. Circle your best $\mathcal{D}$ or d on each line.

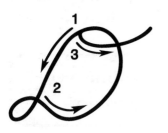 

David

dad

dip

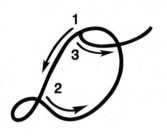 

Trace and write. Circle your best 𝒟 or 𝒹 on each line.

𝒟 · · · · · ·

𝒟 · · · · · ·

𝒟

Diplodocus

𝒹 · 𝒹 · 𝒹 · 𝒹 · 𝒹 · 𝒹 · 𝒹 · 𝒹

𝒹 · · · · · · ·

𝒹

dot

day

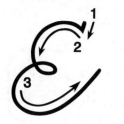 

Trace and write. Circle your best $\mathcal{E}$ or e on each line.

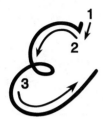 

Ethan

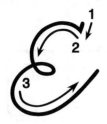 

20 © Chalkboard Publishing

Trace and write. Circle your best $\mathcal{F}$ or f on each line.

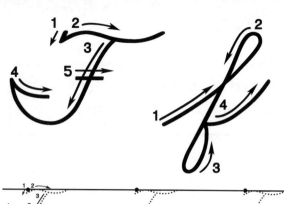

Fred

for

fun

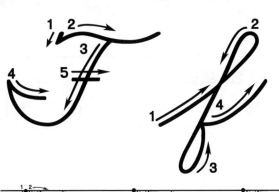

Fukuiraptor

fun

fan

Trace and write. Circle your best *G* or *g* on each line.

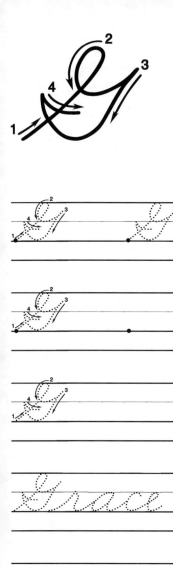 

trace

go

gap

Trace and write. Circle your best *G* or *g* on each line.

Guandong

get

gum

Trace and write. Circle your best $\mathcal{H}$ or h on each line.

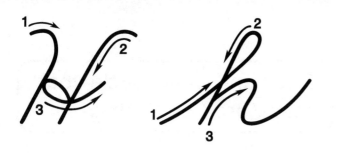

Trace and write. Circle your best 𝓗 or 𝒽 on each line.

𝓗𝓗 𝓗 𝓗 𝓗 𝓗 𝓗

𝓗

𝓗

Harry

𝒽𝒽 𝒽 𝒽 𝒽 𝒽 𝒽

𝒽

𝒽

hop

has

Hadrosaurus

her

him

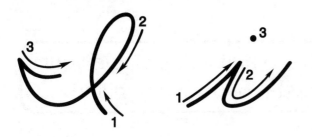

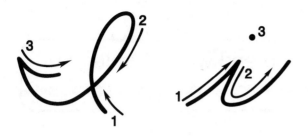

Squamodon

ink

Trace and write. Circle your best ʃ or ɟ on each line.

Trace and write. Circle your best 𝒥 or 𝒿 on each line.

John

jar

jet

Trace and write. Circle your best f or j on each line.

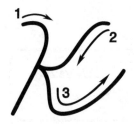 

$\mathcal{K}$ $\mathcal{K}$ $\mathcal{K}$ $\mathcal{K}$ $\mathcal{K}$ $\mathcal{K}$ $\mathcal{K}$

$\mathcal{K}$

$\mathcal{K}$

$\mathcal{K}$erin

k k k k k k k

k

k

knee

key

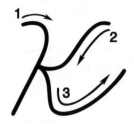 

Trace and write. Circle your best $\mathcal{K}$ or k on each line.

$\mathcal{K}$ $\mathcal{K}$ $\mathcal{K}$ $\mathcal{K}$ $\mathcal{K}$ $\mathcal{K}$ $\mathcal{K}$

$\mathcal{K}$

$\mathcal{K}$

Kotasaurus

k k k k k k k

k

k

kayak

kiss

Larry

lap

log

© Chalkboard Publishing

© Chalkboard Publishing

Trace and write. Circle your best $\mathcal{M}$ or m on each line.

$\mathcal{M}$ m m m m m m

$\mathcal{M}$

$\mathcal{M}$

Michael

m m m m m m

m

m

map

mom

Trace and write. Circle your best $\mathcal{M}$ or m on each line.

$\mathcal{M}$ m m m m m

$\mathcal{M}$

$\mathcal{M}$

$Maiasaura$

m m m m m

m

m

mat

men

n n n n n n

n

n

nancy

m m m m m m m

m

m

nut

meat

n   n   n   n   n   n

n

n

nodosaurus

m   m   m   m   m   m   m

m

m

map

mour

O   *O*   *O*   *O*   *O*   *O*

O

O

China

o   *o*   *o*   *o*   *o*   *o*   *o*

o

o

oat

old

Trace and write. Circle your best $\mathcal{P}$ or p on each line.

Trace and write. Circle your best $\mathcal{P}$ or p on each line.

$\mathcal{P}$ $\mathcal{P}$ $\mathcal{P}$ $\mathcal{P}$ $\mathcal{P}$ $\mathcal{P}$ $\mathcal{P}$

$\mathcal{P}$

$\mathcal{P}$

Petra

p p p p p p p

p

p

pet

pig

Protohadros

pay

pop

Trace and write. Circle your best Q or q on each line.

Trace and write. Circle your best Q or q on each line.

Quinn

quiet

quack

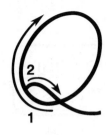

Trace and write. Circle your best Q or q on each line.

Quipalong

quiy

queen

Trace and write. Circle your best $\mathcal{R}$ or r on each line.

$\mathcal{R}$ $\mathcal{R}$ $\mathcal{R}$ $\mathcal{R}$ $\mathcal{R}$ $\mathcal{R}$ $\mathcal{R}$

$\mathcal{R}$

$\mathcal{R}$

Ryan

r r r r r r r

r

r

roll

red

Trace and write. Circle your best *R* or *r* on each line.

R *R* *R* *R* *R* *R* *R*

R

R

Rugops

r *r* *r* *r* *r* *r* *r*

r

r

rip

roar

Trace and write. Circle your best 𝒮 or 𝓈 on each line.

Trace and write. Circle your best 𝒮 or 𝓈 on each line.

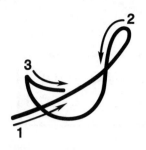

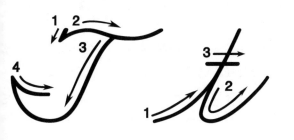

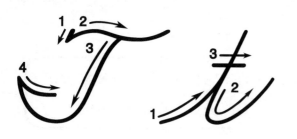

Taylor

tap

the

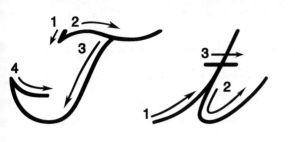

$\mathcal{T}$ $\mathcal{T}$ $\mathcal{T}$ $\mathcal{T}$ $\mathcal{T}$ $\mathcal{T}$ $\mathcal{T}$ $\mathcal{T}$

$\mathcal{T}$

$\mathcal{T}$

Trodon

t t t t t t t t

t

t

toy

tag

© Chalkboard Publishing

𝒰 𝒰 𝒰 𝒰 𝒰 𝒰 𝒰 𝒰

𝒰

𝒰

Uma

𝓊 𝓊 𝓊 𝓊 𝓊 𝓊 𝓊

𝓊

𝓊

up

us

Utahraptor

use

under

Trace and write. Circle your best $\mathcal{V}$ or n on each line.

𝒱

𝒱

𝒱

Victor

𝓃

𝓃

𝓃

nan

navy

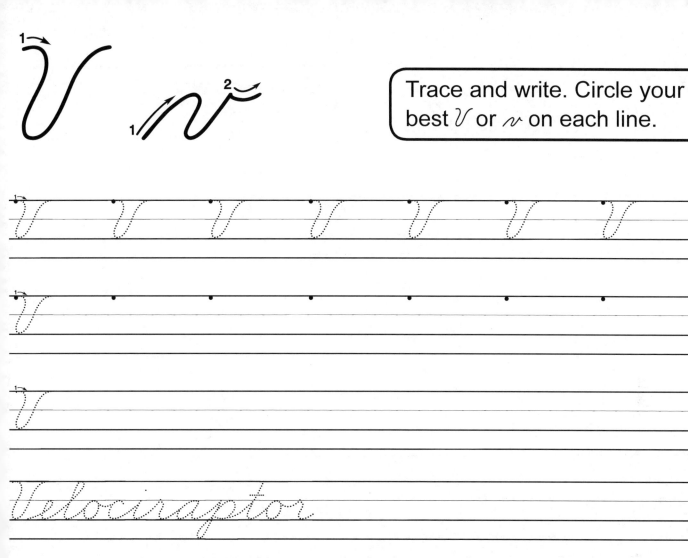

Trace and write. Circle your best *V* or *n* on each line.

Velociraptor

net

your

Wendy

wrout

who

W W W W W W W

W

W

Wulatelong

w w w w w w w

w

w

wet

wan

Karen

x-ray

xylophone

© Chalkboard Publishing

$\mathcal{X}$ $\mathcal{X}$ $\mathcal{X}$ $\mathcal{X}$ $\mathcal{X}$ $\mathcal{X}$ $\mathcal{X}$ $\mathcal{X}$ $\mathcal{X}$

$\mathcal{X}$

$\mathcal{X}$

Xenoceratops

x   x   x   x   x   x   x   x   x

x

x

aztec

atops

Trace and write. Circle your best $\mathscr{Y}$ or y on each line.

Yelana

yak

you

Trace and write. Circle your best *Y* or *y* on each line.

Y Y Y Y Y Y Y

Y

Y

Yandusaurus

y y y y y y y

y

y

yarn

yell

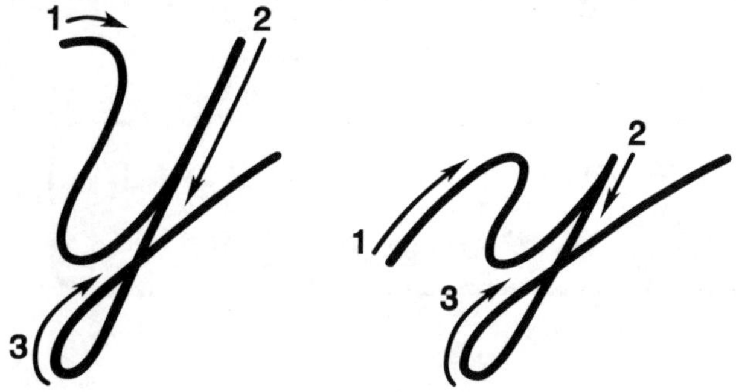

Trace and write. Circle your best *Z* or *z* on each line.

Trace and write. Circle your best Z or z on each line.

Trace and write. Circle your best *Z* or *z* on each line.

More Writing Practice—Provinces and Territories

Alberta

British Columbia

Manitoba

New Brunswick

More Writing Practice—Provinces and Territories (continued)

Newfoundland and Labrador

Northwest Territories

Nova Scotia

Nunavut

More Writing Practice—Provinces and Territories (continued)

Ontario

Prince Edward Island

Québec

Saskatchewan

Yukon

More Writing Practice—Cities

Brandon

Calgary

Charlottetown

Edmonton

Iqaluit

More Writing Practice—Cities (continued)

Moncton

Montréal

Ottawa

Québec

Regina

More Writing Practice—Cities (continued)

Saint John

Saskatoon

St. John's

Summerside

Toronto

More Writing Practice—Cities (continued)

Vancouver

Victoria

Whitehorse

Winnipeg

Yellowknife

Writing Practice—Number Words

one

two

three

four

five

six

seven

eight

nine

ten

Writing Practice—Number Words (continued)

eleven

twelve

thirteen

fourteen

fifteen

sixteen

seventeen

eighteen

nineteen

twenty

Writing Practice—Number Words (continued)

thirty

forty

fifty

sixty

seventy

eighty

ninety

hundred

thousand

million

billion

Writing Practice—Colours

Fill the spots with the correct colour. Trace and write the colour name.

yellow

blue

red

orange

green

purple

pink

brown

Writing Practice—Colours (continued)

Fill the spots with the correct colour. Trace and write the colour name.

beige

gold

silver

black

grey

turquoise

white

peach

Writing Practice—Days of the Week

Trace and write the days of the week.

Monday

Tuesday

Wednesday

Thursday

Friday

Saturday

Sunday

Writing Practice—Months of the Year

Trace and write the months of the year and colour the pictures.

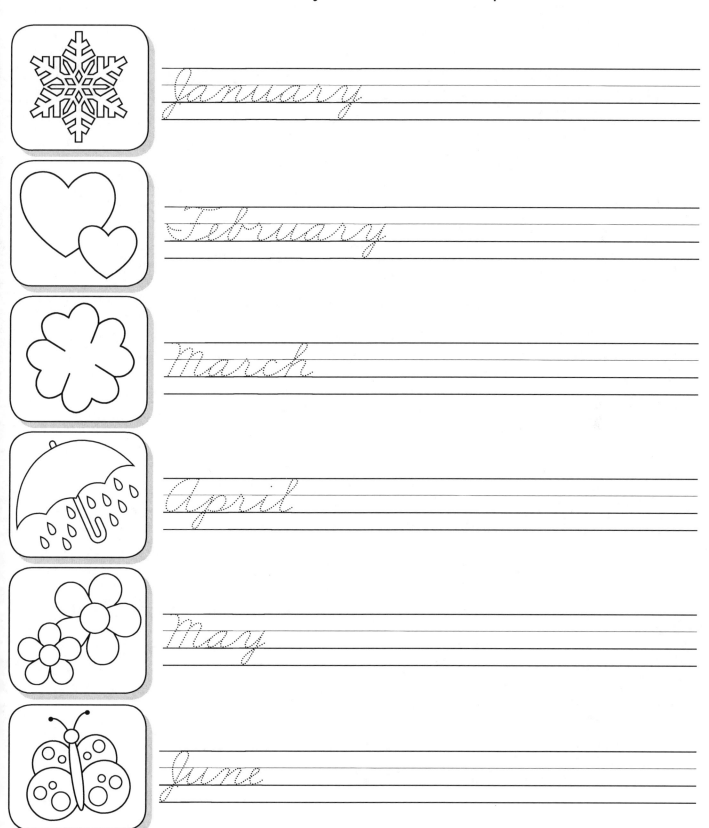

January

February

March

April

May

June

Writing Practice—Months of the Year (continued)

Trace and write the months of the year and colour the pictures.

July

August

September

October

November

December

Writing Practice—Seasons of the Year

Trace and write each season word. Write a list of activities you like to do for each season.

Cursive Writing Challenges

Colour in the box as you complete a cursive writing challenge.

Copy your favourite poem.	Copy the lyrics to one of your favourite songs.	Write a poem.
Copy a recipe.	Create an invitation to an event.	Copy five proverbs or sayings.
Copy some of your favourite jokes.	Make a list of your favourite books.	Write a letter to a friend or relative.
Make a grocery list.	Copy five riddles you enjoy.	Copy the rules of a game.

Practise Your Signature

Collect Signatures

Cursive Writing Rubric

Name: _____ **Date:** _____

	Emergent	Developing	Capable	Mastered
Letter Shape	Few letters are formed correctly.	Some letters are formed correctly.	Most of the letters are formed correctly.	Almost all letters are formed correctly.
Slant of Letters	Little uniformity in slant of letters.	Some uniformity in slant of letters.	Good uniformity in slant of letters.	Excellent uniformity in slant of letters.
Connection to the Line	Few letters are within the lines.	Some letters are within the lines.	Most letters are within the lines.	Almost all letters are within the lines.
Letter Spacing	Few letters are spaced appropriately.	Some letters are spaced appropriately.	Most letters are spaced appropriately.	Almost all letters are spaced appropriately.
Neatness	Few letters/ words are legible.	Some letters/ words are legible.	Most letters/ words are legible.	Almost all letters/ words are legible.
Daily Work	Cursive writing skills learned are rarely applied to daily work.	Cursive writing skills learned are sometimes applied to daily work.	Cursive writing skills learned are usually applied to daily work.	Cursive writing skills learned are consistently applied to daily work.

Observations:

_____

_____

_____

Letters Requiring Practice:

Completion Chart

Great Penmanship!

Keep it up!

Penmanship Award

Keep up the good work!